WHAT ARE JOBS AND EARNINGS?

MARCIA AMIDON LUSTED

Britannica
Educational Publishing

IN ASSOCIATION WITH

ROSEN
EDUCATIONAL SERVICES

Published in 2017 by Britannica Educational Publishing (a trademark of Encyclopædia Britannica, Inc.) in association with The Rosen Publishing Group, Inc.
29 East 21st Street, New York, NY 10010

To see additional Britannica Educational Publishing titles, go to rosenpublishing.com.

First Edition

Britannica Educational Publishing
J.E. Luebering: Executive Director, Core Editorial
Mary Rose McCudden: Editor, Britannica Student Encyclopedia

Rosen Publishing
Heather Moore Niver: Editor
Nelson Sá: Art Director
Brian Garvey: Designer
Cindy Reiman: Photography Manager
Heather Moore Niver: Photo Researcher

Library of Congress Cataloging-in-Publication Data
Names: Lüsted, Marcia Amidon, author.
Title: What are jobs and earnings? / Marcia Amidon Lusted.
Description: First edition. | New York : Britannica Educational Publishing in
   association with Rosen Educational Services, 2017. | Series: Let's find
   out! Community economics | Includes bibliographical references and index.
Identifiers: LCCN 2016000283| ISBN 9781680484014 (library bound : alk. paper)
   | ISBN 9781680484090 (pbk. : alk. paper) | ISBN 9781680483772 (6-pack :
   alk. paper)
Subjects: LCSH: Labor market—Juvenile literature. | Employment (Economic
   theory)—Juvenile literature. | Occupations—Juvenile literature. |
   Economics—Juvenile literature.
Classification: LCC HD5706 .L876 2016 | DDC 331.1—dc23
LC record available at http://lccn.loc.gov/2016000283

Manufactured in the United States of America

Photo Credits: Cover, interior pages background image mangostock/Shutterstock.com; p. 4 Kris Timken/Blend Images/Getty Images; p. 5 Goodluz/Shutterstock.com; p. 6 © iStockphoto.com/BraunS; p. 7 © iStockphoto.com/sshepard; p. 8 Teodora D/Shutterstock.com; p. 9 Monty Rakusen/Cultura/Getty Images; p. 10 © iStockphoto.com/RyanJLane; p. 11 © iStockphoto.com/monkeybusinessimages; p. 12 Monkey Business Images/Shutterstock.com; p. 13 Hero Images/Getty Images; p. 14 © iStockphoto.com/Susan Chiang; p. 15 © iStockphoto.com/Pamela Moore; p. 16 Alys Tomlinson/Cultura/Getty Images; p. 17 Kevin Trageser/The Image Bank/Getty Images; p. 18 Cultura RM Exclusive/Seb Oliver/Cultura Exclusive/Getty Images; p. 19 Kathrin Ziegler/Taxi/Getty Images; p. 20 JGI/Tom Grill/Blend Images/Getty Images; p. 20 Guido Mieth/Moment Select/Getty Images; p. 22 U.S. Navy/Getty Images; p. 23 © iStockphoto.com/mediaphotos; p. 24 © iStockphoto.com/Yuri Arcurs; p. 25 Goodluz/Shutterstock.com; p. 26 mangostock/Shutterstock.com; p. 27 racorn/Shutterstock.com; p. 28 Morganka/Shutterstock.com; p. 29 Africa Studio/Shutterstock.com

CONTENTS

Working for a Living

What is a job? People are doing jobs in their communities every day. They might be firefighters, store clerks, or teachers. They may take care of children, design buildings, or drive trucks. Many people receive money for doing their jobs. Others, such as moms who stay at home to take care of

Firefighters have one of the most important jobs in a community.

COMPARE AND CONTRAST

Some people start out in a job, discover they love it, and make it into a career that they do all their lives. What is the difference between a job and a career? How are they similar?

their kids, or people who volunteer to help the elderly, might not be paid. But they are all doing different kinds of jobs.

Jobs are an important part of an economy. An economy is all the things that go into making, selling, and using goods and services.

Some people volunteer to help the elderly, without expecting payment for their help.

Working Together

Communities need the products and services that people provide through their jobs. Communities also need the exchange of money between buyers and sellers. People with jobs also buy homes and pay taxes. Taxes are fees paid to governments. They are used to build schools and roads and to provide services. People with jobs help their community, and even their country, function.

Families in a community need to have jobs so that they can pay taxes and buy homes. This helps make the community function.

◀◀

Schools rely on money from taxes so they can provide a good education to students.

Sometimes there are not enough jobs for everyone in a community. Stores close if people can't afford to buy things. Without a balance of buying and selling, the community cannot have a good economy. With fewer people paying taxes the community must cut back on services like police and firefighters. School budgets may also be cut. People may even move away to find jobs elsewhere.

A **budget** is a plan for using money. It helps people decide how much money can be spent and how it will be spent. Families, businesses, and governments all use budgets.

Jobs in History

Once people traded work for food or goods. This is called barter. Someone who had a load of firewood might trade with someone else who had a pig. People performed jobs for each other in trade too. A blacksmith might shoe a horse in exchange for a carpenter repairing his front door.

People used to trade goods, such as a load of firewood, for the other things that they needed.

COMPARE AND CONTRAST

Compare the barter system with buying, selling, and working for money. Do you think the barter system would work today? Why or why not?

When people stopped being able to live on what they could grow and trade for, they began to take jobs to earn money. Many people began working in factories. They worked long hours for low pay. If they were sick or injured, they lost their jobs. Finally the government passed laws to improve working conditions. Some jobs still do not pay enough for people to buy the things they need, however.

Factories today must provide a safe work environment for their employees.

What's in a Job?

Jobs help the people who do them. They earn the money they need to live. This money might be actual cash, a paper check that they can cash at the bank, or an automatic deposit into their bank account. They also learn new skills. These skills might help them get other jobs later on. People also gain a feeling of self-respect and responsibility when they do a job well.

Some people receive paychecks that they can cash at a bank. Others have their pay deposited directly into their bank account.

THINK ABOUT IT

Some people do jobs without expecting to get any pay. They volunteer in schools, nursing homes, and animal shelters. What might people get from volunteering?

Workers learn how to do their jobs through on-the-job training, which teaches them new skills while they work.

Employers who pay people to do work for them also get something in return for the money they pay people to do the jobs. They get help in making products or providing services. This helps their business stay healthy and even grow. A strong business means that the employees will continue to have jobs, too.

Looking for a Job

A **vocational school** teaches people skills for certain jobs. They might learn to be mechanics, plumbers, or electricians. They can also learn special skills, like how to fix computers.

People need and want jobs. Some people go to college or a vocational school to learn how to do certain jobs. Doctors and engineers go to school for many years to learn their jobs. Others find advertisements for jobs online or

One way to learn new skills is by attending college or a vocational school.

in newspapers and learn how to do the work on the job. Some people start their own business, like a store, and work there.

People may lose their jobs if they do their work poorly or if their company cannot afford to pay them. This can create a bad economic cycle. People without jobs cannot buy goods and services. The businesses that make those goods and services then cannot survive, either.

Owning a business is very satisfying, but it is also a big responsibility.

TRAINING

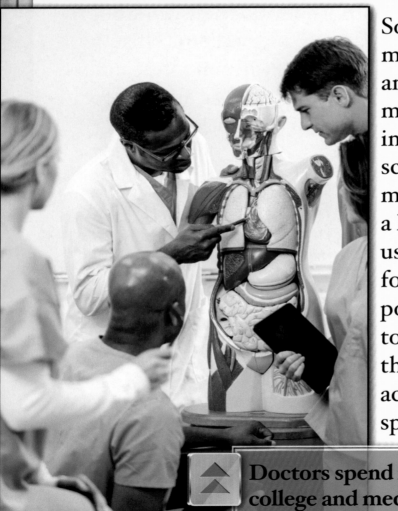

Some jobs require many years of college and training. A doctor may spend eight years in college and medical school plus many more years working in a hospital. A teacher usually goes to college for at least four years. A police officer has to go to college for four years, then attend the police academy. They learn special skills and have

Doctors spend many years attending college and medical school before they can treat people.

COMPARE AND CONTRAST

Doctors and lawyers are usually paid much more to do their jobs than teachers and police officers. Are their jobs more important? Why or why not?

to be physically fit. Many people keep learning even after they have jobs.

Because they need so much training, these kinds of jobs often pay more than other jobs. The people who do them are very important to the community because they have these special skills and knowledge. They are valuable to the economy because of the services they provide.

Police cadets attend classes and go through physical fitness training before becoming police officers.

MAKING THINGS AND GROWING THINGS

Some jobs focus on creating and making things. They include craftsmen like carpenters, builders, and people who make clothing or work in a factory that makes cars or computers. They also include electricians and plumbers, who can help build new homes and other buildings or repair old ones.

Craftspeople may learn their jobs by working with someone who is already a master in that field.

THINK ABOUT IT

Many producers do jobs that used to be done by people at home, like growing food and making clothes. Why do you think this would be very hard for most people to do now? Does it have to do with where most people live today?

Farmers are also producers. They grow food for people and animals to eat. They raise animals. They might also produce wool or cotton for clothes or trees for building. There are also producers who bake bread or make cheese. They take what farmers grow and make it into products that people need.

Bakers make pastries and bread for customers using ingredients like flour and sugar.

17

Can I Help You?

Hair stylists provide a service that most people can't do for themselves.

Another important kind of job has to do with providing a service that people need. Most people cannot fix their own cars or cut their own hair. They need other people to do these jobs for them. In a restaurant, cooks and servers are needed to make and bring customers their food. If someone needs a coat mended, they go to a tailor.

A bike shop provides a service by fixing bikes. It also provides goods, such as new bikes and accessories.

People who own stores provide a service by selling certain things such as food or clothes or hardware. Housekeepers, hotel employees, and house painters also provide services.

IT'S ALL ABOUT THE ARTS

Many people have special talents in music, art, and writing. They find jobs that use their talents. They play the piano, sing, conduct symphony orchestras, or play in a rock band. Other

THINK ABOUT IT

Movie stars and famous singers who are known around the world make huge amounts of money. Artists who perform mostly in their own communities usually do not. Why do you think this is true?

A talented musician can make money by performing or by writing music.

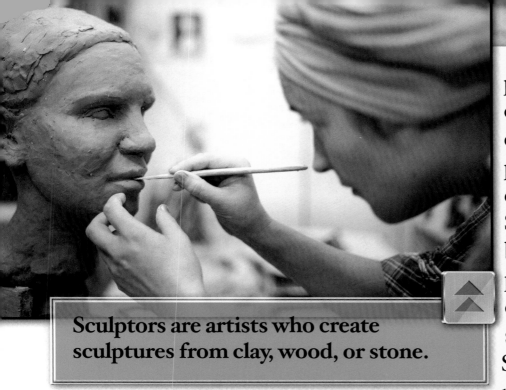

Sculptors are artists who create sculptures from clay, wood, or stone.

people lead church choirs or play church organs. Some paint beautiful paintings or create sculptures. Still other people act on stage or in movies. Or perhaps they write books, poetry, or magazine articles.

Jobs like these contribute different kinds of arts to the community. They provide something beyond the basic needs of everyday life. Some people who work in the arts make a great deal of money. Others are not paid as much, but it is important to them that they love what they do.

SERVING THEIR COUNTRY

Some people have jobs that serve their community and country. But these jobs might require them to live elsewhere. People who **enlist** in the army or the navy may live far from home. They may even fight in wars and risk their lives to protect their homes, their states, and their country.

When someone joins the military they **enlist**. When they enlist, they agree to join the military for a certain amount of time.

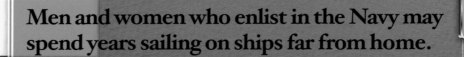

Men and women who enlist in the Navy may spend years sailing on ships far from home.

Government employees may work in local, state, or federal government jobs.

Many people work at government jobs. They may work in their town or city government. They may be elected to serve at the state level. Some are elected to serve in Washington, D.C., representing their state. There are also people who have government jobs in places like national parks.

For How Long?

Some people love their job and keep it for most of their working lives, especially if they had years of school or training. Others have many jobs. This might be because they like trying new things. Sometimes the company or business they work for no longer needs them. Some

People who really love their job may work in the same place for many years.

companies go out of business, and their employees lose their jobs.

If people are interested in their work, they are more likely to keep their job. It is important for people to think about whether they would like a job before they start the job. They might do an internship to try out a job. There are also tests that people take to show them what kinds of jobs they would do well. People who join the military often take these tests.

An **internship** is a temporary job with a company. It gives the intern a chance to try out a job and also gives them training. Some interns are paid, but others are not.

An internship is not only a way to learn new skills. It is also a way to try out a job.

New Job, No Job

One way jobs are created is when a new company or business opens and needs workers. It might hire people who already have experience in that business or people who need training. Communities like to have new businesses open and hire people. It helps the economy by creating new jobs. It also attracts people to live there.

A new business creates jobs because it needs to hire many people, both new and experienced.

When people lose jobs they can get help from their community or state. They can receive unemployment payments. This is money from the government to help them pay their bills until they find a new job. Many communities also have organizations to help people find jobs, get training, and receive education.

Community and state agencies can help people find jobs.

Everything Working Together

In our modern society, people cannot survive without some means of earning money. They need both jobs and earnings to help support themselves as well as their families. Communities cannot survive without people doing jobs. These jobs provide services people in the community need and want. Jobs also provide

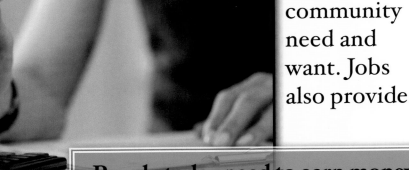

People today need to earn money in order to survive.

COMPARE AND CONTRAST

A salary is a set amount of money that someone gets every week for doing his or her job. Other jobs pay a certain amount of money for every hour worked. Is one way of getting paid for a job better than the other? Why or why not?

People and their communities work together to create a healthy economy.

products people in the community buy. Jobs help bring tax dollars to the community as well.

Jobs and earnings work together. People who work, and the communities they work and live in, make a healthy economy possible.

Glossary

account A sum of money deposited in a bank.

advertisement A public notice or announcement, such as for a job vacancy.

afford To be able to pay for something.

agency A part of a government that manages projects in a certain area.

blacksmith A worker who shapes iron (as into horseshoes) by heating it and then hammering it into shape on an iron block.

civilization A large group of people who share certain advanced ways of living and working.

conditions The circumstances affecting the way people live or work.

crop A plant or animal or plant or animal product that can be grown and harvested.

deposit Money placed in a bank to keep it safe.

elderly Of or relating to later life or older persons.

elected To select someone by vote for an office, position, or membership.

electrician A person who installs, operates, or repairs electrical equipment.

employee One who works for another for wages or a salary.

engineer A person who designs, builds, or maintains engines, machines, or public works.

fired When someone is dismissed from their job.

function To serve a certain purpose, or to work.

orchestra An assembly of musicians that performs musical works written for a group.

plumber A person who puts in or repairs the pipes and fixtures involved in the distribution and use of water in a building.

taxes Money that people and businesses pay to support public services.

training To teach someone in an art, profession, or trade.

unemployment The state of not having a job.

volunteer Someone who offers to do something without being paid.

FOR MORE INFORMATION

Books

Bozzo, Linda. *Community Helpers of the Past, Present, and Future*. New York, NY: Enslow/Bailey Books, 2010.

Bullard, Lisa. *Ella Earns Her Own Money*. Minneapolis, MN: Millbrook Press, 2013.

Callery, Sean. *Branches of the Military*. New York, NY: Scholastic Books, 2014.

Catalano, Angela. *Community Plans: Making Choices about Money in Communities*. New York, NY: Rosen Publishing, 2005.

Fischer, James. *Earning Money: Jobs*. Broomall, PA: Mason Crest, 2009.

Kalman, Bobbie. *Helpers in My Community*. New York, NY: Crabtree Publishing, 2011.

Silverstein, Alvin, and Virginia Silverstein. *Poop Collectors, Armpit Sniffers, and More: The Yucky Jobs Book*. New York, NY: Enslow, 2010.

Websites

Because of the changing nature of Internet links, Rosen Publishing has developed an online list of websites related to the subject of this book. This site is updated regularly. Please use this link to access the list:

http://www.rosenlinks.com/LFO/jobs

Index